The Brave Women of World War II

Biography for Children

Children's Women Biographies

BABY PROFESSOR

EDUCATION KIDS

Speedy Publishing LLC
40 E. Main St. #1156
Newark, DE 19711
www.speedypublishing.com

Copyright 2017

When the nations went to war in World War II, it was not just young men marching off to fight each other far away. The war was near at hand, and not just men but women did their part as well.

Here are some stories about women warriors of World War II—people who gave up careers and studies, and risked their lives for their nation…and sometimes lost those lives.

What Can a Woman Do In a War?

In the middle of the 20th century, most men, who ran most governments, still felt women were less intelligent, less strong, and less capable than men.

In some countries like Italy, the government said the best contribution women could make to the war effort was as "baby factories". In many countries at the start of World War II in 1939, women could not vote or hold public office.

In countries on the front lines of battle, the situation was so desperate that armies took all men and women they could find. In Russia, for instance, women served as members of artillery crews, often firing the guns, as well as nurses, clerks, and couriers, and in other support roles. Across all countries, over 100,000 women had front-line combat roles.

In many countries, women both served in the military and took over jobs on "the home front" so that the men could go off to war. On the following pages we will learn about these jobs and some of the amazing women that did them.

United States

In the United States, a famous poster of "Rosie the Riveter" celebrated women taking over factory jobs to free up men for military work. Women assembled everything from bombs to bombers. They learned how to operate turret lathes and blowtorches. Women's participation in the war effort had a major effect on advances in the status of women in the United States in the years after World War II.

Land Girls operating a tractor

United Kingdom

To keep farms productive, many city women went to work as "Land Girls". They operated tractors, planted and harvested crops, built dykes to control water flow, and in general kept England's rural economy operating.

Another major contribution was the "Bletchley Circle", four women who worked on a top-secret project to crack the German military codes. The Germans had a code-creating machine that defied normal code-breaking attempts. One of the women found a pattern in German messages that allowed the British to build a machine that could read the codes. Being able to read the orders to German land and naval units gave the Allies a great, and secret, advantage in the war.

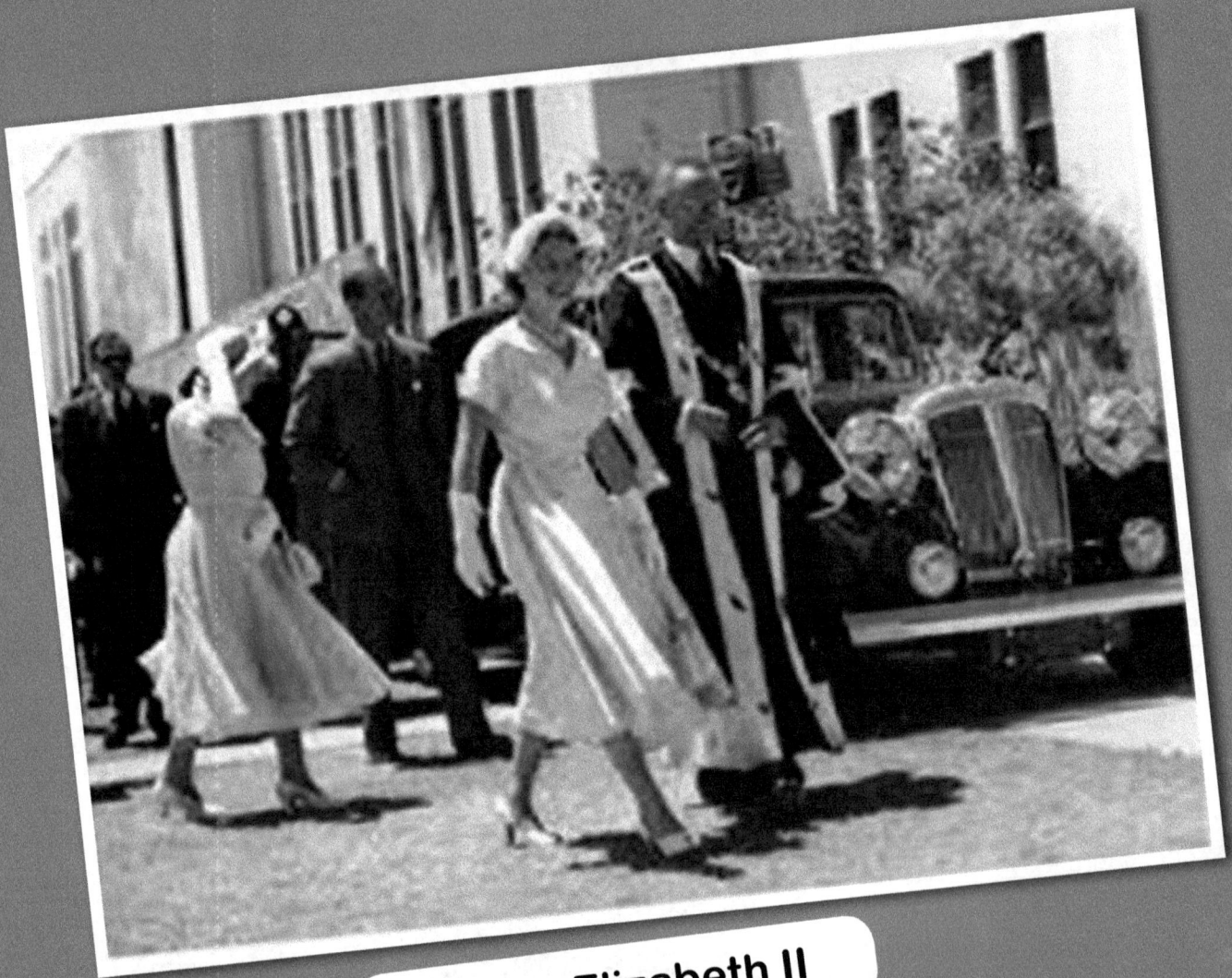

Queen Elizabeth II

Women and men from all levels of society contributed to the war effort. Queen Elizabeth II, as a young woman, served as an ambulance driver during World War II.

Germany

Although some women served with anti-aircraft units, most women worked in support roles. By 1945, women held 85% of war-related support jobs like clerk, accountant, interpreter, laboratory worker, and administrator.

Romania

The Romanian air force featured the "White Squadron", an air ambulance service from 1941-1943 that had mostly women pilots and crew.

Yugoslavia

About two million women joined Yugoslavia's AFZ (the Antifascist Front of Women) during the war. They operated hospitals, schools, and some town and city governments. Over 100,000 women served in the Yugoslav army fighting against both Italian and German forces.

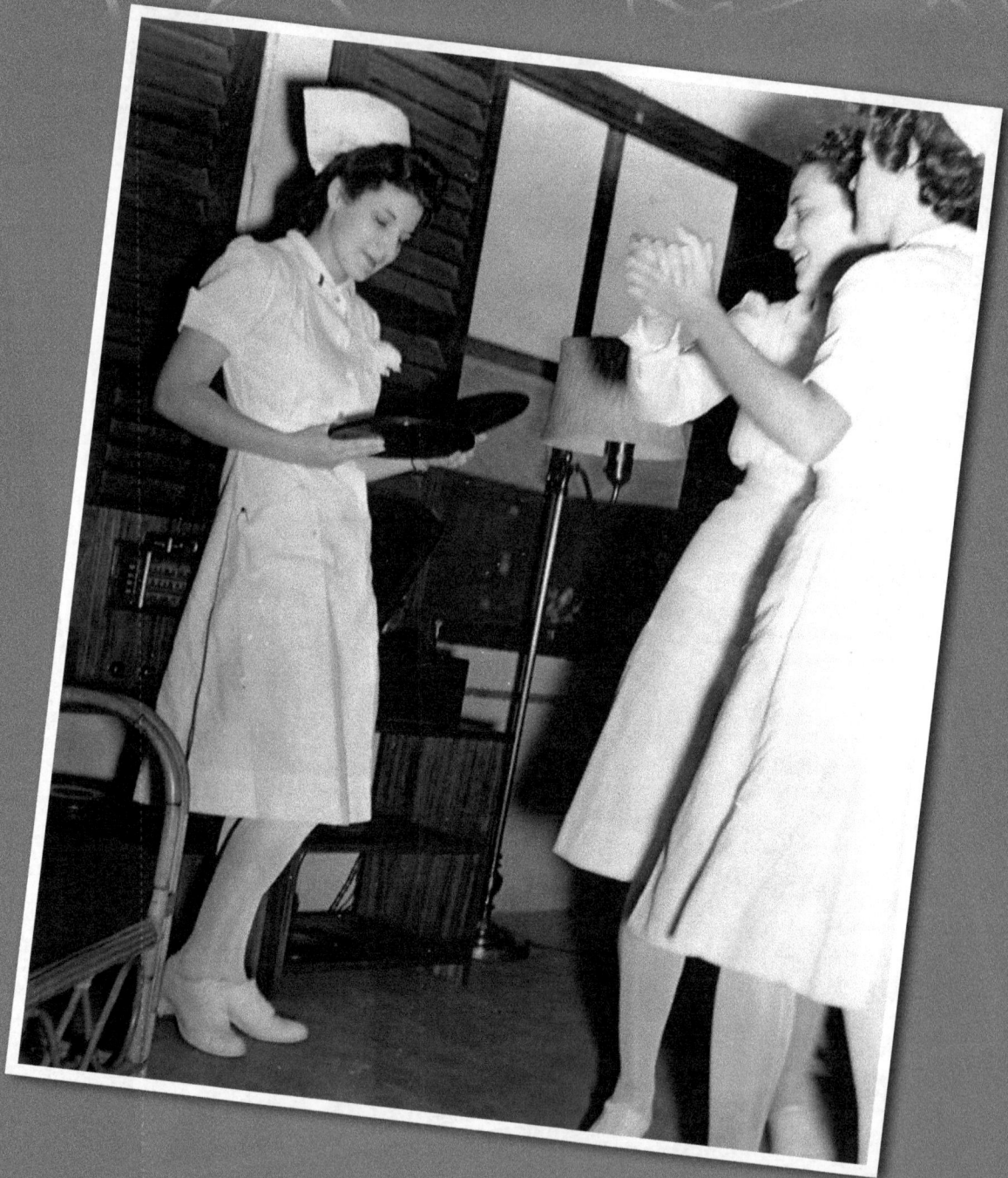

Women warriors

Here are some remarkable women who risked life and liberty during World War II:

Queen Wilhelmina

When Germany invaded the Netherlands, Queen Wilhelmina wanted to stay and take part in the resistance. She was convinced to go into exile in England. From there she broadcast talks that gave inspiration and hope to the Dutch people, and was head of the Dutch government-in-exile.

Queen Wilhelmina

Zoya Kosmodemyanskaya

When Germany's invasion of the Soviet Union drew close to the capital, Moscow, Zoya was eighteen years old. She volunteered to be part of a guerrilla group that would operate behind German lines. She took part in an operation to burn a village and set land mines. The Germans captured her, but could get no information from her. After she was executed, she became a symbol of Soviet resistance to invasion.

Felice Schragenheim

Felice was an ordinary German woman. She tried to leave Germany before the start of World War II, but did not succeed. During the war, her official job was with a Nazi government newspaper. Secretly, she fed information to the German resistance forces. She also helped many Jewish people escape from Germany. She herself was arrested in 1943, and died in a concentration camp.

HIER WOHNTE
FELICE
SCHRAGENHEIM
JG. 1922
DEPORTIERT 1944
THERESIENSTADT
AUSCHWITZ
GROSS ROSEN
???

Violette Szabo

Violette's family was English and French, and although she grew up in England she was fluent in both languages. She married an officer of the French Foreign Legion. When he died in battle, Violette joined the British Special Operations Executive (SOE) to avenge him.

She worked in occupied France to hamper the Germans by blowing up bridges and rail lines, and as a courier. She helped organize networks of resistance fighters. Even after she was captured, Violette worked from within prison camps to help the resistance and pass information to spies. She organized an escape attempt, which failed, and she and others were executed in early 1945.

Barbara Lauwers

Born in Czechoslovakia, Barbara moved with her husband to the United States in 1941. In 1943, once she became a citizen, she joined the U.S. military. She worked with German and Czech prisoners of war who did not support the Nazis.

She taught them how to spread rumors and false news that would lower German morale and weaken the Nazi war effort when they were sent back to Germany. She helped to bring over 600 Czech soldiers to the Allied side.

Barbara Lauwers

Lise Børsum

Lise was the wife of a doctor in German-occupied Norway. She smuggled many Jews from Norway into neutral Sweden, sometimes hiding them in her own house until it was safe for them to move. She was arrested in 1943 and spent the rest of the war in a concentration camp. After the war, she continued her work helping the civilian victims of wars around the world.

Princess Noor-un-nisa Inayat Khan

Noor was a pacifist from India who strongly supported Indian independence from the United Kingdom. But when World War II started, she worked as an intelligence operator for the British to help fight the Germans.

Vysokopetrovsky Monastery in Moscow
Princess Noor-un-nisa Inayat Khan's Birthplace

She and her family were living in France as the war started, and barely escaped to England. She joined the SOE and trained as a spy. She operated a secret radio network in France to get information to resistance fighters, and to send intelligence to the British. She was arrested in 1943, escaped once, and was recaptured and executed.

Lyudmila Pavlichenko

Lyudmila, a college student in Kiev in the Soviet Union, was already a skilled competitive shooter before the start of World War II. She became part of a unit of 2000 women snipers, of whom only 500 survived the war. In 1942, Lyudmila killed over 300 German soldiers, including almost 40 snipers. She was wounded by an exploding mortar shell and spent the rest of the war training other women to be snipers.

Christine Granville

Christine was born Krystyna Skarbek, the daughter of a Polish count. At the start of World War II she was living in Ethiopia. She contacted the British and volunteered to sneak back into Poland to help organize resistance groups and spy networks there. She was arrested in 1941 but managed to escape. She went to Egypt, under British control, and took on her new identity. She then trained in sabotage and as a paratrooper.

She parachuted into France as part of the Normandy Invasion in 1944. Her assault area was overrun by the Germans, and she had to walk 70 miles to safety. Christine then worked in the French Alps to convince French supporters of the Nazis to give up and even to join the Allies. She had a remarkable rate of success, taking many risks in the process. For example, she revealed who she was to French officials to convince them to release to her prisoners that were supposed to be sent to German prisoner-of-war camps.

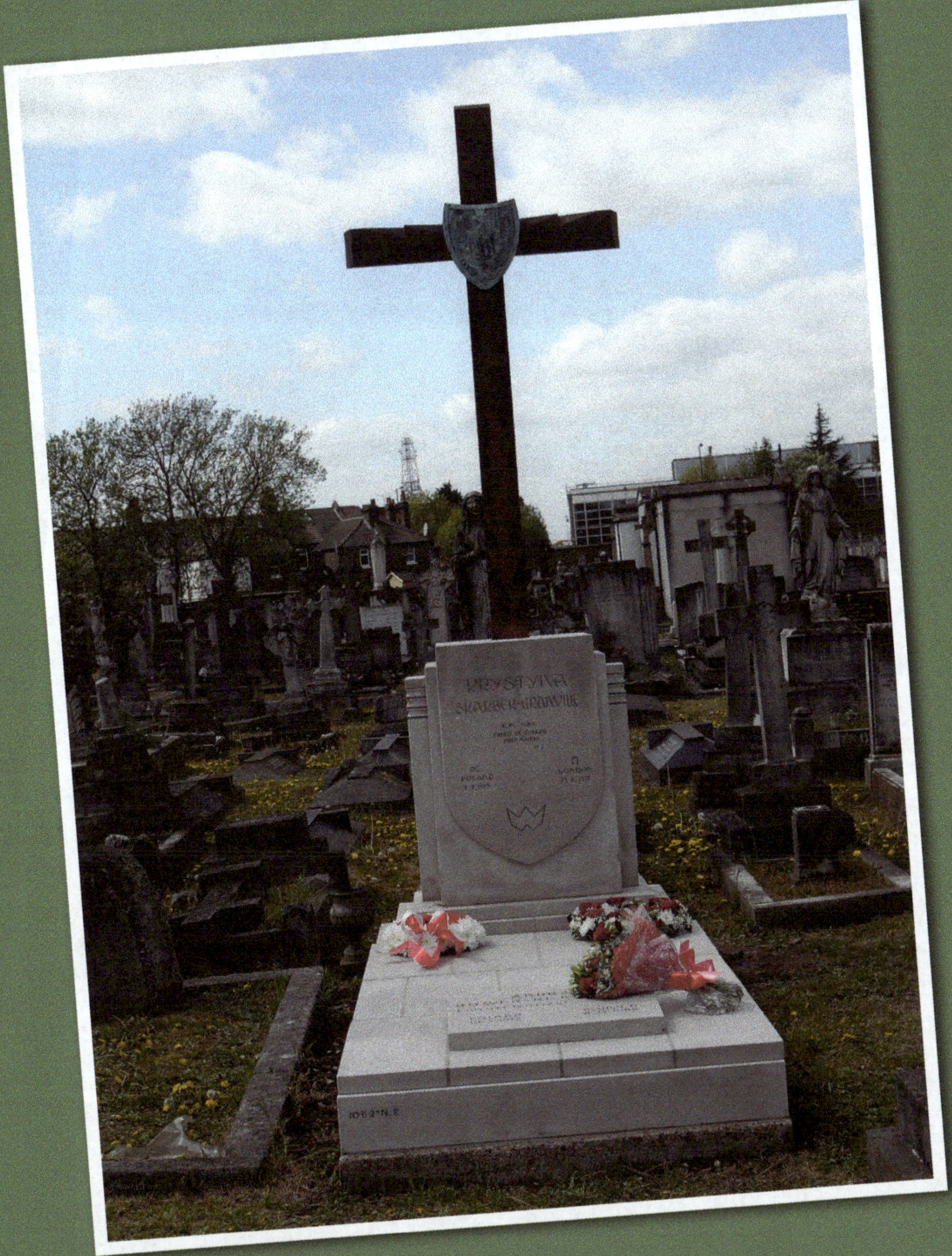

Ruby Bradley

Ruby was a career nurse in the U.S. army, and was administering a military hospital in the Philippines. When the Japanese invaded the Philippines, she and a doctor tried to hide in the hills. Betrayed and captured, she spent three years at her former base, which was now a prison. She worked as a nurse, performed surgery, and saved many lives and worked to reduce suffering even though she had a desperate shortage of supplies and equipment.

Nancy Wake

Nancy, born in New Zealand and raised in Australia, was living in France at the start of World War II. She first worked with the French resistance, hiding fighters and getting supplies for them. She then escaped to England and trained in weapons and as a parachutist. She returned to France as a behind-the-lines fighter. The Germans called her "The White Mouse" because she was able to sneak up on them, launch her attack, and then slip away.

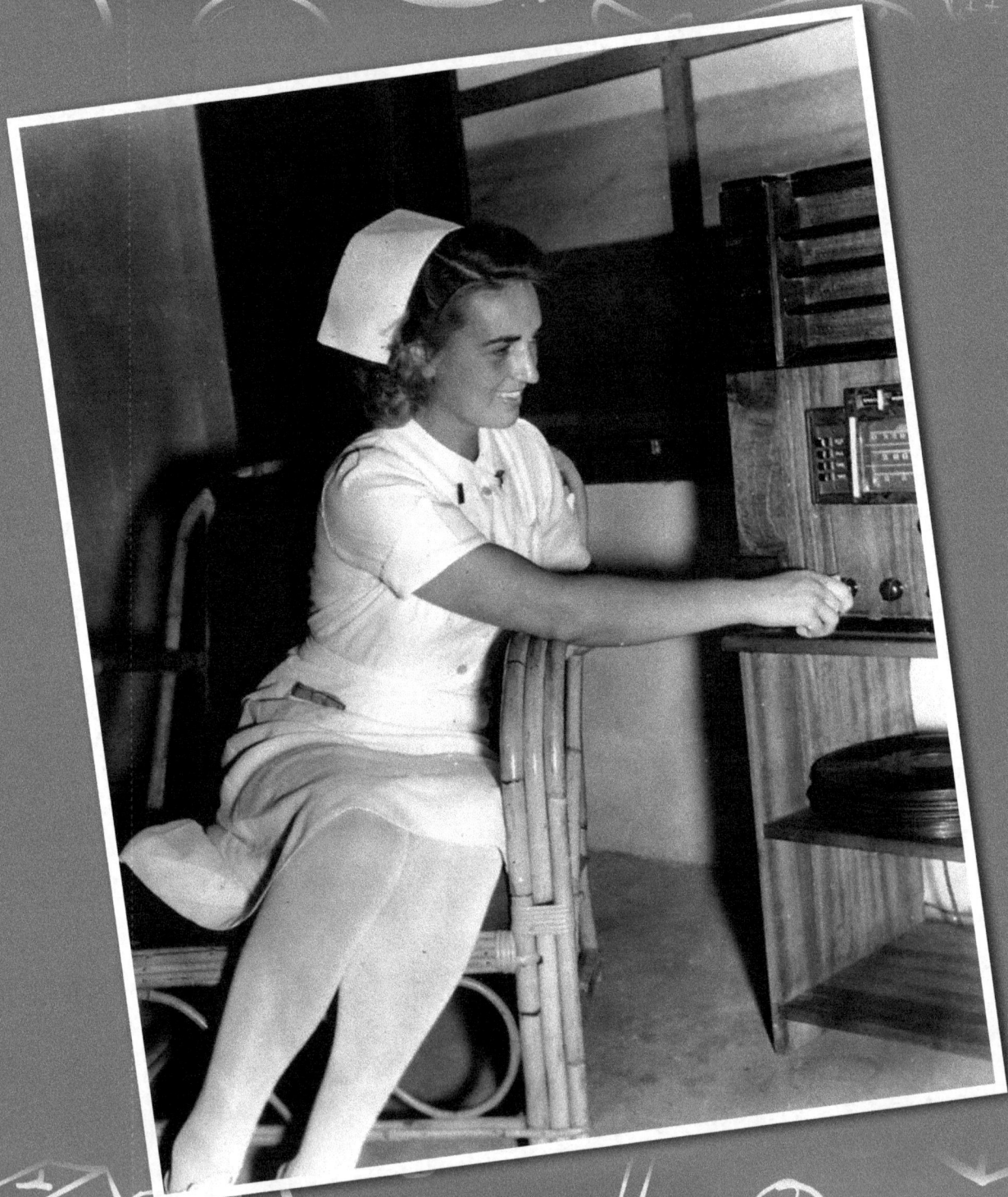

Heroes all around us

In dangerous times, all good people have to step up and do their part, as these women did. Read other Baby Professor books to learn about other heroes in times of peril.

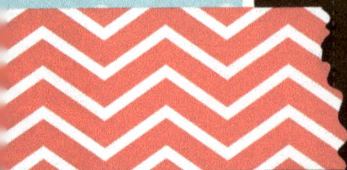

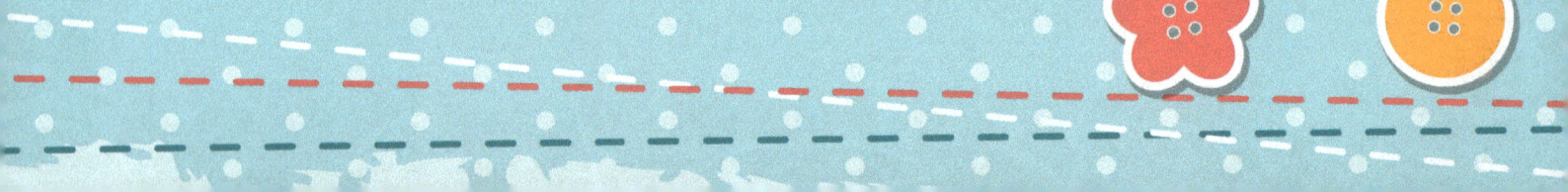

Visit

BABY PROFESSOR
EDUCATION KIDS

www.BabyProfessorBooks.com

to download Free Baby Professor eBooks
and view our catalog of new and exciting
Children's Books

Milton Keynes UK
Ingram Content Group UK Ltd.
UKHW051140030924
447802UK00003B/273

9 798869 416728